Real Estate Investing

A Beginner's Guide to Buying and Selling Property the Right Way

Table of Contents

Introduction

I want to thank you and congratulate you for deciding to read the book Real Estate Investing: A Beginner's Guide to Buying and Selling Property the Right Way. This book will provide you with everything you need to know about how to invest in real estate in a way that will make you profitable and give you more financial freedom for years to come. You will not only learn about why investing in real estate can be one of the most rewarding decisions a person can make, but also become aware of the general risks associated with real estate investing. By investigating the different types of real estate investing that are available to you as an entrepreneur, you will be able to choose which type of investment you want to make and how much risk you want to take on as an up-and-coming investor.

If you are reading this e-book in hopes that you can "get rich quick" by seeking to capitalize in the real estate industry, you have already made a bad investment. While making gobs of money is a possibility within the real estate industry, making money overnight is not likely. Real estate investing takes time and often takes the prowess of multiple people to accomplish profitable goals. Additionally, if you rush through the process of learning the intricacies of what real estate investing involves, you are likely to make mistakes and end up losing money instead of making smart investments that will be beneficial to you. In order to make money, you have to spend money; however, it cannot be overstated how important it is to do the research necessary before spending any cash or assets in order to maximize your return. Take your time and you will be ahead of many investors who have already been working in the real estate market for many years.

This book contains proven strategies on how to become a truly reputable real estate investor. In addition to discussing the benefits and risks involved when venturing into real estate investment, this book seeks to specifically highlight ways to be successful with multiple type of real estate investment. Once you pick the type of investment (or investments) that you are interested in making, the techniques and advice in this book will serve as the starting point you need to implement the right strategies from the jump. With this book as your guide, you will feel confident navigating the potentially unfamiliar territory you have an interest in entering.

Here's an inescapable fact: you will need some money and courage in order to become a successful real estate investor. Similar to working in the stock market, a common saying within the real estate investment industry is to start as young as you can. If you are young now, you have the time to learn and invest your money wisely. If you are older, know that there are many people who are younger than you already in the industry. This makes it even more important that you work diligently to absorb the necessary information within this ever-growing industry.

If you do not develop your knowledge of the real estate market, there is a chance that you will never profit from your real estate investments as much as is possible. Even if you are not positive that you are going to invest in real estate after reading this book, knowing the market in which your current home investments operate can help avoid getting taken advantage of as a homeowner. This means that even if you are simply a homeowner and not a real estate investor, you can still benefit from the information provided in this book. Additionally, if you currently rent a home and do not yet own a home, the tips found in this book will allow you to start thinking about how buying a home sooner rather than later could benefit you financially.

It's time for you to become an amazing real estate investor! Don't delay learning more about these investment strategies. Let's get started!

Chapter 1:
Why You Should Invest in Real Estate

While it has been scientifically proven that money does not lead directly to a person's happiness, a different way to look at this redundant and almost cliché saying is to think about it in terms of an individual's freedom. Having more capital gives you more options, and of course the goal of any individual in today's society is to be able to make decisions that are autonomous of being tied to the need to work or a need to borrow money from an institution that profits from accrued interest. Having more cash gives you the ability to provide more for your family and feel safer within the turbulent atmosphere of both the national and international economy. A great way to actualize these desires for freedom and safety is through the investment of real estate property. While making real estate investments can be a great way to either supplement income or have these investments be the basis for a business in its own right, it needs to be emphasized up front that there is responsibility that accompanies this type of venture. This becomes even more apparent upon looking at recent events in history.

The Call to Not Let History Repeat Itself

In 2008, the national stock market crash sent ripples of loss and crisis throughout the entire world. This crisis is important for the particular subject of real estate investing because the crash was primarily caused by the actions of lenders and brokers within the housing market sector. It is the consensus of many economists and lawmakers alike that private entities that were not subject to federal regulations were the ones who were preying on people who did not understand how the real estate market worked much less how the concepts of lending and interest would ruin their lives. More than half of the people who private real estate investors would target were those people who had bad credit scores and who were forced to pay higher interest rates than those people with satisfactory credit scores. Their bad credit scores alone were enough to indicate that these individuals might stop paying their mortgages and the high interest rates associated with them, but it almost seemed like the real estate investment groups behind the lending of this money were hoping for defaults to occur. Profiting as much as was possible, the investors involved in the 2008 housing crisis had little regard for how the individual homeowners who made up their investments would pay for lavish houses that they couldn't afford. The investors saw their bottom line and were blind to what their gain meant to those who were less knowledgeable about their ability to pay back loans. These naïve homeowners had the odds stacked against them from the beginning.

This should matter to you, the hopeful real estate investor, because while learning to navigate the tricky nuances of the world of real estate investing you should always be mindful of the past. Unless you choose to invest in rental properties, you want to be careful about to whom you lend your money. Of course, you are reading this book because you want to make a profit, but what matters most is that you are not swindling people in order to make this possible. Depending on where this venture leads you, you may or may not be confronted with a situation where you will have the chance to take advantage of someone financially. If this situation were to occur, the best advice available would be to think about yourself prior to reading this book. You sought this type of book out because you are seeking greater freedom in your life. If you are to gouge someone financially, even if you are merely being coerced by others in your investment circle to do so, you are indirectly impeding the financial freedom of an individual. Before implementing any of the strategies presented in this book, be honest with the people who are giving you their money. They are trusting you to provide them with factual and transparent information.

While the responsibility involved in making the decision on whether or not to lend someone money should not be understated, there are plenty of reasons why it could be greatly beneficial for you to set yourself up now as a real estate investor. Let's move towards a lighter subject and take a look at how real estate investing might be exactly what your wallet needs.

The Many Benefits to Making Real Estate Investments

Positive Cash Flow

Particularly when you, as an investor, decide to purchase a multi-family home in hopes of renting it out, you are able to secure your assets through the lease agreements that you have with your tenants. As long as you are able to find tenants who typically pay their rent on a yearly or six-month basis, you should be able to consistently have a positive cash flow that offsets the cost of the mortgage on the house. For example, say that your first investment property has a mortgage payment of $1,270 per month. If you own a duplex and each family pays $1,000 to occupy the residence each month, you are left with a net profit margin of $730 every month. This serves to not only give you some extra cash, but also serves to yield a higher return than if you hadn't bought the house and that money was sitting in the bank. It's not likely that the initial money that you put down for the house would yield the same return on interest if it were just sitting in the bank gathering dust.

Noticing the Value of Inflation

Overall inflation has made it increasingly harder to buy goods because the purchasing power of money has decreased over time. Inflation occurs when a government decides to print more money in hopes of stimulating the economy. The idea is that if there is more paper money to be spent, goods will be bought more quickly and businesses will stay healthy; however, in practice, this leads to an overall depreciation of currency. As people have more money and buying power, the owner of a product or service sees this and increases the price of the good or service in order to maintain its worth amidst a changing currency value. While inflation is generally regarded as a negative, the exact reasons for inflation are the contents of an entirely different e-book somewhere in cyberspace. What is pertinent for the real estate investor to know is that generally when inflation occurs, the price of real estate also jumps with it. This means that while the individual consumer suffers through the realities that inflation brings with it, the real estate investor thrives because the cost of housing is positively correlated with rising inflation.

Asset Appreciation

Because there has been increasing amounts of inflation bogging down the economy over time, the purchasing power of the dollar in particular has become severely limited compared to its power in the past. Again, similar to the tendencies of inflation and its positive effect on the cost of a home for a property investor, the same can be said about the value of the physical home that an investor purchases over time.

While other types of asset-oriented investments are riskier in the sense that it can sometimes be a gamble as to whether or not the asset will appreciate in value, it is proven that houses typically appreciate, rather than depreciate, over time. This is a solid reason why investing in real estate could be great for you.

Asset Capitalization

In conjunction with asset appreciation over time, the multiple physical aspects of a house also have a concrete value. For example, the land on which the house is built, the structure itself, and the income that it is currently producing for you can all prove to be significant sources of value if you ever were to consider selling your income property. Asset capitalization and appreciation are two concepts that are an advantage to a real estate investor, regardless of which type of approach you choose to take. We will discuss the various approaches you can take within the real estate investment market in the following chapters, but the multiple ways that a home gathers value is another reason why real estate investments are safer than other investment types.

Pride

A less tangible, yet still relevant reason why it would be advantageous for you to invest in real estate is the pride associated with the venture. Unlike other forms of investment where the portfolio is primarily kept between the flaps of a bulky envelope, the portfolio of a real estate investor lines the streets of a neighborhood and can help other individuals actualize their home-owning dreams. Even though other people will be occupying the residencies of your asset, part or all of that property belongs to you. Especially if you are not only looking to become a real estate investor but also do your own home improvement projects, the pride felt from finishing a kitchen or a bathroom is something that can help to achieve an overall sense of happiness. In this way, investment properties are not only a potential source of freedom, they're also a potential source of enjoyment and indicator to others of your palpable success.

Chapter 2:
Seven Common Mistakes Beginner Investors Make

It can be extremely exciting when you first start investing in real estate. Due to this feeling of excitement, it might be the tendency of a novice real estate investor to rush into an investment or not think enough before making a decision. These fast choices can later be extremely detrimental to an investor's portfolio far into the future. This chapter will focus on common mistakes that beginning investors make, in hopes that in being aware of these errors, you can avoid them. A long-lasting and smart real estate investor knows what causes failure within the industry, and works in a way that not only avoids lazy tendencies but also is profitable. Avoid the mistakes presented in this chapter, and you will be one step closer to growing your wealth over time.

Mistake 1: Using Real Estate Investing as a Get-Rich Quick Scheme

One of the biggest mistakes a new real estate investor can make is thinking that by investing in real estate, he or she is bound to get rich quick. This simply is not the case. Of course, we have all been exposed to commercials and advertisements that claim real estate investing is a quick trick way to become rich overnight, but these advertisements usually want the viewer to buy a product in exchange for some sort of educational tool or "shortcut". Because you are reading this book, it is safe to assume that you're looking to educate yourself on the topic of real estate investing, rather than purchase some expensive course. The ability to "get rich quick" is something that does not exist in the world of real estate marketing; however, many people new to the field seem to forget this and make hasty decisions based on this assumption.

Mistake 2: Working Without a Roadmap

Many new investors tend to look for properties instead of looking for opportunities. Let me explain. It's not uncommon for investors to first buy a house that he or she loves, and then figure out what to do with the property. Ideally, this process should be the other way around. An investor should be looking to find a house that already fits into his or her investment plan, instead of falling in love with a property and buying it simply because it has pretty windows or a spacious lawn. Along these same lines, the investor needs to realize early on that the most important aspect of an investment should not be whether or not the investor loves the property. Instead, the investor needs to think about whether or not the property has the potential to be maximally profitable in the future. Planning after you purchase a property instead of planning out your investment strategy and then seeking a property that fits within this plan is a major mistake and is a reflection of emotional buying instead of smart buying.

Mistake 3: Miscalculating What a Property is Worth

Almost as important as planning out your investment prior to making your purchase is understanding how much value your investment has in the eyes of your buyers or renters. If you aren't aware of what your buyers and renters want when they look to buy a home or rent an apartment, how can you invest in a property that you are sure will sell? It's also important to do your calculations properly so that you don't pay too much. You don't have to spend a fortune on outside information in order to figure out what it is your potential tenants want. Spending time on websites such as Zillow or MLS can help you to figure out how much homes are going for in the area in which you're looking to invest. Additionally, once a home sells, these online sources advertise both the asking price and the actual selling price, as well as additional information that is helpful to an investor. These details include how long the property has been on the market and how much the price of the house has gone down during its time on the market. Sources that cost more money but may also be beneficial to you include hiring professionals such as an appraiser or real estate agent. For more formal training, the option also exists for you to attend classes about the principles of valuation through the Associate of Realtors.

Mistake 4: Going it Alone

Even if you know that you primarily want your investments to be made solely by you, without bringing in other investors, it is short-sighted to think that you will be able to successfully make investments without the help of others. The types of people that you should form relationships with include people in the following fields: a home inspector, a real estate agent, an appraiser, and a closing attorney. Depending on how wide the area is in which you are going to be buying property, it might be a good idea to seek people out in these categories in multiple locations. This way, you can cover a greater geographical area. If you already know people within these industries, you're off to a good start. If you are jogging your memory and can't think of anyone, it should be relatively easy to find people who will want to work with you. These people ultimately want their business to grow. As an investor, you'll be perceived as a promise of more business in their eyes.

Mistake 5: Misjudging the Cost of Repairs

In addition to knowing people within certain financial and property-related fields, it's also good to know people who work in the construction industry. If you know that you are going to want to repair the homes in which you invest, you are going to want to form relationships with people like roofers, electricians, and heating and air conditioning specialists. Of course, these relationships will be less crucial if you are not looking to buy and sell rental properties. In thinking about this, word of mouth is a good way to find reputable people who stand out within their industry and who work in the area in which you're looking to buy property. Ask around and you're sure to find the right people.

Knowing people in the construction and repair fields will help to lower repair costs over time. If someone knows that you're an investor and that you're buying a property that requires repairs relatively frequently, he or she will be more likely to provide you with lower rates because of the promise of consistent work. Additionally, it might also be beneficial for you to generate a repair estimation system. You are bound to spend more than you anticipate on at least one of your repair projects. Developing an accurate estimation for your repairs will help you to be better aware of how much a certain type of project is going to be. This will take some practice, but over time your estimation for repairs will become more accurate.

Mistake 6: Not Educating Yourself

Can you imagine what would happen if you or someone you knew decided to work in the car maintenance industry without taking the time to learn about how to repair a muffler or an engine? Being a real estate investor involves a lot more than simply writing checks, and yet one of the most detrimental mistakes that a new investor is more likely to make is entering the investing marketplace with very little knowledge of how the industry operates. Real estate investing isn't necessarily simple. There are both winners and losers within its ranks. The competition involved in real estate investing is what makes it both risky and exciting, and you can give yourself an edge over the foolhardy investors whom you're competing against by cracking open a book or two. You don't have to spend a lot of money on real estate education. Of course, you are educating yourself now by reading this book, but you should also consider taking out books from the library that dive even deeper into these topics.

Mistake 7: Having Only One Exit Strategy

If you are going to make investing in property a business, you will need to have multiple investments being in transaction at once. If you only focus your energy on one property at a time, waiting until closing one deal before starting another, your property investment "business" will be in reality, more like a hobby. Giving yourself the opportunity to work on multiple investments simultaneously will allow your profit margins to expand and maximize. Additionally, the more properties you work with, the more experience you'll get in the process. Along these same lines, it's also important to have more than one exit strategy once a deal has been made. If your only plan is to fix up a house and then sell it, what will you do if you find that the house isn't selling? Some other options include offering the potential renter a lease-to-own option, where he is she is working towards owning the home through their monthly rent payments. Or, you could choose to involve another investor and sell the property to him or her at a below-market price. Of course, you obviously want to make a profit from selling this property, but if it is looking like the house may not sell at all, this may be your best option.

All of the mistakes that were highlighted in this chapter should be remembered so that you are less likely to make these mistakes in your own investment portfolio. Additionally, a great tip that can help to mitigate all of the mistakes outlined in this chapter is to overestimate your time and budget before you buy a property. While doing your calculations, consider doubling the amount of time and money that this investment will take. If your calculations lead you to the conclusion that you will still make a profit if this project turned out to be much more expensive and much more time consuming than you originally anticipated, it is likely that you are making a sound investment. Now that you've read about the mistakes that should be avoided when investing in real estate as a whole, the remainder of the book will focus on the different types of real estate investment options that are available to you. After you learn about each one, you'll be able to choose which ones are most suitable for your individual investment strategies.

Chapter 3:
You're the Landlord –
How to Invest in Rental Properties

The first type of investment that we're going to look at is one that involves little in terms of knowing investment jargon or technical terms. This type of investment is investment into rental properties. We've already discussed how this type of investment is anything but a "get rich quick" strategy, but this type of investment can be a great way for a young or inexperienced investor to dip his or her toe into the investment property pool. The other chapters will focus on ways to invest that require more of a financial than physical commitment. Here, we will look at the steps that are necessary to take and aspects of the buying process that you should be thinking about before purchasing your first rental property.

Tip 1: Know How Much Money You Need

It sounds fabulous on the surface – as a landlord, you will have the ability to pay for the mortgage on the house with the money that your tenants give you each month. If you invest correctly and calculate your mortgage payment right, you could also ideally find yourself making a profit off of the monthly rent checks that you receive. Being a landlord, however, is not cheap. The first step to owning a rental property is being aware of how much money is necessary. Typically, a bank will not give you a loan for the mortgage on an investment property without your agreement to put down twenty to twenty-five percent of the cost of the mortgage. For example, let's say that you find a property that costs $150,000 but you talk the owner down to $100,000 (imagine if you could talk the owner down $50,000 in real life!). This means that you will need to give the bank $20,000 in order for them to approve the mortgage. This amount might seem like chump change, but this is only for a single property. If you're trying to start an investment business through the purchasing of real estate properties, then you are going to need at least $20,000 each time you buy a house. It's safe to assume that the actual property you're going to want to purchase will cost a lot more than $100,000 in total. Additionally, the twenty percent that you put down are not the only costs that are required when buying a home. Closing costs average around $3,000, home owners insurance averages around $1,000 for the year, and unknown repairs for your home should average around $10,000.

These high costs make it not only crucial that you know that you have the funds available, but also that you are sure that you are truly interested in becoming a landlord.

An additional tip that involves knowing how much money you need is also recognizing that once you have an investment property, the possibility exists for you to refinance your home with no interest. While this ability varies state-to-state, refinancing will give you the opportunity to have more immediate funds available. You will be able to use these funds for whatever you want, such as for repairs or for investing in more property.

Tip 2: Investing in the Right Place

After you've determined whether or not your current funds match what is required to buy an investment property, your homework isn't finished. While we've already discussed the benefits offered by sites like Zillow or MLS to find the average cost of properties in a given geographical area, it's also important to recognize why a house is being valued at a certain price. For example, if you come across a house that you think is a bargain, you need to look at the factors that surround the house before immediately buying the property. If the property itself looks nice but also looks like it is being underpriced, some other aspects to consider is the school system that encompasses the house and the crime rates for that given area. These would be reasons to not buy the property because it will be harder to rent or sell in the long term. Even if you personally don't care about the school system or the crime rate, your tenants are going to care. This is especially true is the property is three or four bedrooms and there is a chance that a family will live there.

Along the same lines of knowing what the surrounding area of the property is like, it is also suggested that you only buy in areas that are familiar to you. It's advice that you don't invest in out-of-state property. It is much easier to buy something when you've grown up around it and have a sense of what the culture is like. Knowing the culture surrounding a property will give you a better idea of what type of property will be successful and what won't. It's important to also realize that this type of knowledge is not necessarily something that you can read out of a book. For example, in thinking about how many rooms you want your property to be, you should consider the types of people who live in the area. If you were looking for properties in a location that included a college, it would be extremely beneficial for you to know which streets were most populated with students who attended the school. You would want to purchase property on those streets, rather than on streets that were harder to make sales on. If they are college students, you would ideally be looking for three or four bedroom apartments that would complement a college student's budget and lifestyle. It would arguably be foolish to buy a one bedroom apartment in a college town, because the amount of potential renters who will want a one bedroom apartment are fewer than those who are looking to live with their friends.

Tip 3: Start Small

One of the best ways to figure out whether or not real estate investing is something to which you are going to be truly dedicated is to start small. Your first investment property probably shouldn't be a rundown Victorian castle. Rather, it would be smart to begin your investment endeavors on one or two bedroom apartments that require little in terms of repairs. This is easier said than done, especially when the price of a fixer-upper property can sometimes persuade you towards feeling like can easily learn how to become the next Tim Allen on Home Improvement. But if you invest in something small to start out with, your mortgage payment will be cheaper and that will manifest itself in less money being needed at the start of the investment. At first, it might also be helpful to start your investing with a partner, to cushion the cost of repairs, initial costs and the process of finding tenants. Additionally, a good word of advice to remember is that condominium homes, while they look advantageous because of their relatively small size and the fact that the yard is already maintained by an outside source, these homes usually require a higher percentage of the cost of the home up front. It is widely accepted that condominiums are more difficult to sell than regular homes.

Lastly, the discussion of a "short sale" should be addressed here. A short sale is when the selling price is less than what is actually owed on the property. Often, this occurs when a homeowner goes into bankruptcy and can no longer afford a mortgage payment. The bank essentially owns the property at this point. While the selling price is typically lower than other properties in the surrounding area when this happens, there are many factors involved when navigating how to successfully capitalize on this type of sale. Ironically, while the name "short sale" suggests that a transaction of this nature will be quick and painless, it can take months before the bank is ready to go through with the transaction. If you are confronted with the opportunity to purchase a home through a short sale, a good idea is to research what it entails heavily before proceeding. That way, you can be sure you are making the right decision.

Tip 4: Figure out the Right Rent

Determining how much to charge your tenants can require some real thought. Of course, everyone wants to maximize their return on their rent, but at the same time it's important to recognize how much people are willing to pay within a locale. Additionally, the rent that you charge your tenants should definitely be enough to at least cover the cost of at least the mortgage of the property, if not more. Other factors to think about are monthly sewage costs, garbage collection costs, and down payments. The amount of rent you're going to collect also depends on the type of home that you are offering. It is generally understood that the cost of a one bedroom is usually more than the cost of a two or three bedroom home, because a single person living somewhere is getting more square foot per their dollar. While you certainly want to get the most for your property, it has to be realistic. People have a sense of when they're being taken advantage of.

Tip 5: Know the Worth of a Good Tenant

The last tip for how to successfully begin owning rental property is to understand the value of a good tenant. First and foremost, the largest cost to a landlord is property vacancy. Keeping your tenants happy can help to ensure that they're looking to continue renting your property far into the future. This will give you financial security. These people are your customers and every business man or woman wants to keep their customers happy. Another way to think about a tenant is to consider what type of person you want living in your investment property. While this is not a strict rule, it can be largely assumed that someone with more money, who has a good job and a lot of career-oriented responsibilities, will probably be a better tenant than someone who has low income and will struggle to keep payments consistent. While this may seem like it's a harsh way to look at a person, it is a reality that a landlord must consider.

Lastly, it is important that you are aware of the type of relationship that you want to form with your tenant. If you don't have the firm title of "manager" and the property that the tenant is renting is more like a converted house than an apartment complex, the tenant might perceive you to be more of a friend than as someone in charge. Tread this line carefully. If a tenant begins to think that you're more of a friend than an authority figure, he or she might become more lenient on when or how much they pay you. A tenant should understand that there are consequences for not paying on time. You relationship with your tenant should be a reflection of this fact.

Chapter 4:
Collaboration for a Profit – Real Estate Investment Groups

While we discussed how to start investing in rental properties in the previous chapter, another way to consider going into property investment is to invest in real estate through a real estate investment group. Rental properties were the focus of the first chapter because this chapter also involves offering properties to rental property investors once a housing project is completed. The details of this process are the focus of this chapter. First, we will seek to understand what exactly a real estate investment group is, and then we will look at the both the benefits of this type of investment strategy as well as any disadvantages that exist within this category. By being aware of the risks and profitable aspects of this type of investment, you'll be able to make your own decision on whether or not investing in this type of way will be worth it to you.

What is a Real Estate Investment Group?

Also known as a private partnership, a real estate investment group allows an auxiliary investor to buy living space within an apartment complex or condominium through the predefined structure of their company. Imagine that instead of taking the time to find an investment property through a realtor like was explained in chapter one, you find a group of people who are planning to build homes for the same purpose. This would alleviate the challenge of looking for properties with a realtor because the work is already done for you. What's more, this group of people would also promise to find you tenants and resolve any maintenance or repair responsibilities that occur while the tenant resides in the home. Of course, this type of alleviation isn't free. The investment group, in exchange for finding the tenants and handling maintenance costs, claims a portion of the monthly rent proceeds that their investor (or in this case, landlord) collects. The main element of an investment group that makes it appealing to most people is that it allows for real estate investments to be made without the added hassle of having to also manage a property. In this way, a real estate investment group operates similarly to a mutual fund.

A mutual fund is an investment tool that uses funds from many of its members to make investments. While there are many areas in which an investment group can spend its money, obviously for our purposes the objective is to invest in real estate. Instead of each person within the group controlling its own currency, a money manager exists within the groups' ranks who makes investments with the intention of making a profit from the money that's originally put into a venture. This makes it so each person who puts money into the mutual fund's pool either gains or loses money in accordance with how the group is doing. The money manager promises to make investments based on the objectives that the group states in a document known as the prospectus. This legally binding document is filed with the Securities and Exchange Commission. The Securities and Exchange Commission (SEC) seeks to protect the investors that are filed within it and promotes full transparency to the public. Once you file with the SEC, your transactions can be seen by anyone who wishes to access it. The prospectus also explains what a particular investment group will offer to the public in terms of which goods and services are being invested into and therefore are being promoted by the group.

But back to real estate investment groups. These investment groups work similarly to mutual funds in the sense that these investors are not directly working with the tenant, repair people, etc. They leave this to the landlord that they hire. It's important to note that most of these investment groups require that the landlord in question agrees to cover the cost of a potential property vacancy. This means that while the investment group will look for tenants, if there are none to come by, it will be the responsibility of the landlord to pick up this cost. This, while it is a negative for the landlord can be seen as a vehicle of security of the real estate investment group as a whole. Now that you understand the gist of what a real estate investment group is, let's look at how much immediate capital is required for this type of investment.

Pinching Pennies: How Much Does it Cost to Join a Real Estate Investment Group?

As was obvious in the previous section, it's advantageous to be in the actual investment group and not the landlord when dealing with a real estate investment group. It may seem nice to have your tenants found for you and your repairs to be taken care of, but directly owning a rental property in this way makes you more of a property manager and less a real estate investor. Of course, outright purchasing an entire home is much more financially costly when compared to serving in a property management type position with an investment group. Once the choice has been made that you definitively want to go the route of becoming a member of the investment group, it's important to know exactly how much capital is required. Instead of owning shares of a company, (which is the crux of a mutual fund) a real estate investment group allows you to own a share of a physical real estate property. Imagine that there are four real estate investors within a group, and each of them own a stake in a house. This would be the equivalent of each member of the group owning one room of the entire property (if there were only four rooms in the house). Owning the portion of a house will depend on how much the house itself is worth. For this reason, an investment group will usually accept an investor who is willing to spend between $5,000 to $50,000 dollars. It's easy to determine that $5,000 is not enough to cover the cost of an entire property, but the possibility exists for multiple investors to go in on an investment together. If the investments are successful, a member of a real estate investment group can expect to see monthly cash returns on their investment.

Advantages and Disadvantages of Joining an Investment Club

One of the advantages of becoming part of an investment group has already been stated; as an investor, you avoid having to be responsible for the daily upkeep of your investment property. Another advantage that was touched upon is the ability to invest less money than when buying an investment property in its entirety. By pulling its resources together, an investment group is able to lessen the cost and therefore the risk associated with purchasing an investment home. Some additional advantages to teaming up with a group to accrue investment wealth is that this makes it easier to widen your area of investment. When you are the sole owner of a property, the advice is to keep your radius of investment small because of factors such as having knowledge of good school districts and varying crime rates. By joining an investment group, you are able to widen your investment reach because you are not directly managing the property. Additionally, if you are in a club with people who do live in an area that is far from you, he or she can help to find good property managers in the area. Lastly, consider joining an investment club if you are just starting out in the field because they can be a fabulous way to share strategies, get advice, and possibly learn from a mentor. Real estate investment groups can be a great networking resource.

The cons that surround joining a real estate investment club include the categories of money, time and competition. Some of these groups require that the lenders pay upwards of two hundred dollars per month in order to maintain a membership with them. For an investor who is not looking to spend a ton of money, this can prove to be too costly. Not all investment clubs require this type of financial commitment, so it is possible to look for one that requires no monthly fee. In addition to money, the meetings that investment groups have usually last for at least a couple of hours. Depending on how often your particular group meets, this can mean that you have to spend at least two hours a week at a real estate investment group meeting. These days, everyone is busy. It's important to make sure that you want to make this sort of time commitment before participating in an investment group. Lastly, trust is also involved when you join one of these groups. You are opening up to people who potentially want to compete with you financially within the broader scope of the real estate market. It's important to make sure that this type of transparency is something you won't mind. It's impossible to anticipate how long you will be with an investment group you choose. Make sure that you want to be open with its members before you join.

Chapter 5:
Real Estate Investment Trusts

Similar to a real estate investment group, a real estate investment trust also operates similar to a mutual fund, and is typically considered most advantageous for retail investors. First created in the 1960s, it is also considered one of the cheapest ways to add real estate to an investment portfolio. Owning stock of this nature allows the investor to either invest in real estate through the property itself or through the property's mortgage. Either way, a real estate trust is a direct way to involve yourself with an investment. This chapter will look at what exactly a real estate investment trust is, the importance and significance of dividend reinvestment plans (DRIPs) and why you would want to consider this type of investment strategy. We'll also explore some disadvantages to real estate investment trusts.

What Exactly is a Real Estate Investment Trust?

A real estate investment trust (REIT) is a company that both owns and operates its real estate investment. In most cases, this means that the property is one that produces income. For example, real estate investment trusts own properties such as office buildings, apartment complexes, warehouses, hospitals, hotels, and shopping centers. These real estate properties are bought with the intention of developing them as their own entity. They are not typically sold as investments in the future. These types of investments were created in 1960 by the United States Congress. What makes this type of investment attractive is that fact that it is possible to avoid paying income taxes on the properties that are bought through this avenue. To do this, the trust typically makes it mandatory to spend at least ninety percent of its taxable income. These payments are usually made in the form of dividends to their shareholders. One big reason why new investors are usually interested in REITs is because entering this market is less expensive than joining other types of ventures. The average amount of money that an investor needs to join an REIT is between five hundred to twenty-five hundred dollars. In order to fully understand this type of investment structure, an explanation of the dividend reinvestment plan (DRIPs) is necessary.

A Dividend Reinvestment Plan

A dividend reinvestment plan, or DRIP, is an option offered by many corporations that allows the investor to use the money that is given to them towards buying more shares in the company with whom they're already invested. This type of investment plan is also known by many as simply a DRP. While these shares usually cannot be played on the stock market because this money is coming directly from the company itself rather than an outside investor, the advantages to being involved with a DRIP include not having to pay a commission on the share as well as enjoying a discount from the current share price. This discount usually ranges from one to ten percent. This in itself is a great advantage because the cost of owning these shares is lower than if an individual purchased auxiliary shares on the open stock market. The biggest advantage to a DRIP can be seen long term. While the investor is not able to trade these types of shares on the open market, he or she is able to instead reinvest these shares into the purchase of more and more shares. Over time, there is the potential that the total amount of money that the investor sees will be significantly greater than if many shares had not been bought by the individual.

Additionally, when the price of the company's share goes down, you are also able to buy a share from the inside at the same discounted rate. This is also good for the company as a whole because it means that you as a DRIP investor are less likely to sell your shares of the company when the company's share price decreases. This means that not only are DRIP investments less liquid than other types of investments, but they are also a way to ensure that the company that you're invested in is safe for the long term. For this type of investment to make sense, patience and commitment to one specific company are necessary. You obviously would not want to be investing in a company that you don't think offers a good product or service, because with this type of investment strategy you will frequently be buying many shares of this company. The hope is that the returns will increasingly grow over time.

Types of REITs

Now that you are familiar with the broad aspects of an REIT and how a dividend reinvestment plan works, it's time to look specifically at the different types of REITs that exist. REITs are the perfect way to diversify your investment portfolio. It's important to choose the right REIT that will complement what you're looking to do with your tenure as an investor. Let's take a look at the different type of strategies now.

Retail REITs

The first type of REIT that we'll discuss is a retail REIT. This type of REIT includes shopping centers and malls. It's likely that any retail store that you go to is owned by an REIT. These trusts earn their money by charging rent to the retail tenants. This being the case, it's important to choose healthy retail stores when looking to invest in this type of way. Vacancies in retail buildings can be a real inconvenience to fill. If a retail store that you invest in goes bankrupt, the consequences of their bankruptcy will manifest itself in your portfolio's wallet. As a general tip, grocery stores and home improvement stores are seen as safe investments within retail REIT. Another aspect of the retail company itself that should be considered is how well the company is run. If the company you're looking to buy can't take care of itself financially, you may want to reconsider investing in it. Finally, it's important to make sure that the retail economy itself is doing well before you make this type of investment. The last thing you want to do is buy shares in the retail market when its economy is in a slump.

Residential REITs

Residential REITs own and control multi-family properties as well as more standardized forms of housing such as apartment complexes. If you're looking to get into this type of market, it is crucial to your success that you focus your investment energy in areas where the cost to rent an apartment is relatively high when compared to the rest of the country. For example, New York City is a good example of a place where the cost to own an apartment is far greater than the average person's ability to pay for one. Due to this fact, most people are forced to rent instead of own a home in New York City. Because the demand for a rented apartment is high, the landlords in New York City are able to charge higher rent prices. This is a great example of a place where a residential REIT investor should look to invest because there is the promise of a high rate of return. Because of this, REITs are often found in megacities. You should also look at how fast the city's job growth is happening in correlation with how fast the population is growing. More jobs being added to the city's economy means that more people will be migrating there and will need a place to stay. When researching for residential REITs, be on the lookout for cities with low residential vacancy rates and high rental rates. This indicates to an investor that the market is ripe for purchasing property.

Health Care REITs

Health care REITs invest in hospitals, retirement homes and medical centers. The advantages to this type of investment are still unknown, mostly because the way in which these types of businesses are funded vary so greatly from one another. Some of the ways in which these types of places earn money is through private clients and Medicare and Medicaid. It is pretty easily assumed that the more health care that a community requires, the better it will be for the health care REIT. Another reason why the overall wealth that might exist within this category is unknown is because of the flux of the health care system as a whole in the United States.

Mortgage REITs

REITs that are tied to mortgage instead of real estate itself include companies such as Fannie Mae and Freddie Mac. While this may seem like a secure investment type, the reality is that there are many factors that can affect the profitability of this type of investment. For example, if the variable interest rate of a loan increases, the result would be a decrease in the overall value of the REIT mortgage investment. From an investor's perspective, this means that less people would be likely to put their money in this type of trade. It is important to research fully the implications of investing in this type of REIT before committing to a financial transaction within this realm.

Office REITs

As the name suggests, Office REITs invest in office buildings. These types of investments are less risky than the other REITs we've discussed because office buildings usually involve long-term leases. Broadly speaking, it is better to own a few office buildings if you are going to go this route, because this will distribute your risk throughout multiple properties. Other aspects to consider are the unemployment rate in a given area and the vacancy rates for these types of buildings.

In addition to thinking about the fact that you can invest in a trust for relatively cheap, other advantages to this type of investment include higher dividend yields and investment appreciation in the long-term. That being said, if you are looking for a way to gain cash assets quickly, this would not be a good route for you. Lastly, crucial to your success within this category is to only choose to buy stock in something that has a history of strong and experienced management and has been in business for a minimum of five years. If you are going to go into residential REIT, make sure to invest only in those properties that are both great properties and have historically great tenants. With this type of investment being cheaper than the others that we've discussed so far, you should really consider adding it to your investment portfolio.

Chapter 6:
The Ins and Outs of Real Estate Trading

If you've ever been in elementary school and at one point or another found yourself trading snacks in the cafeteria with a friend, you are already sort of familiar with the concept of a "like-kind" exchange. Whether you were aware of it or not at the time, trading in this way benefited both you and your friend without much of a consequence for either of you. In the same way, some real estate investors seek to trade real estate properties with the intent to avoid consequences from the government. To be more specific, real estate trading involves avoiding taxes on investment property until the home is later sold for cash. This chapter will focus on the details of this type of exchange, as well as the high risks that are associated. As will become apparent, the ability to balance along the thin line of what is legal and what is illegal in the eyes of the looming taxman can prove to be a complicated juggling act. Knowing which lines are okay to cross and which lines are potentially jail-worthy can be something that can prove to be life altering when done incorrectly. More so than most of the chapters that we've highlighted, it is particularly important to have an adequate sense of what you're doing before attempting this type of investment.

A 1031 Exchange

The type of "like-kind" exchange that was discussed above is more formally known as a 1031 in the tax world. A 1031 is when one investor's property is exchanged for another investor's property, with the tax on each being deferred until the investment is liquidated at a later time. Only commercial properties can be traded this way. There are ways that a vacation property can be swapped in this manner, but the technicalities surrounding this type of trade are too much for this book. While we will look at other rules that encompass this type of tax shortcut, it is good to know that broadly speaking there is no limit as to how many times you can use a 1031 exchange (when administered properly). The hope from the government's perspective is that you will use this saved tax money to invest in other properties time and time again. When you go to finally liquidate your investments and pay your taxes, you will only be required to pay one tax. If you invest correctly, the amount of money that you pay in taxes will be less than what you accrued over time by waiting to pay them until later. This is how a real estate trading investor makes a profit, but it's also how the government seeks to make theirs. This type of investment is a serious gamble and the details of it need to be understood before using it. Now that it's understood from a basic perspective what real estate trading, and more specifically what a 1031 exchange is, let's look at some rules that limit how this type of tax break can be used.

1031 Exchange Rule 1: Some Personal Property Qualifies

While it was previously stated that residential properties are not allowed to be traded in a 1031 exchange, some personal property such as paintings or antiques do quality as being eligible within the 1031 exchange parameters. It's important to note here that while some personal assets do qualify, assets such as stocks do not. This is important when considering other types of investment strategies that are possible beyond ones that strictly involve real estate.

1031 Exchange Rule 2: The Vague Characteristic of "Similar" Property

The term "like-kind" implies that the values of the real estate being traded must be similar in nature; however, this does not always hold true. For example, there have historically been trades made that have involved a strip mall being traded for the raw land found on a ranch. It's even possible to exchange one type of business for another, such as a salon for an accounting firm. While this seems like the rules within the 1031 exchange are pretty laissez-fare, you have to be sure that the possibility does not exist for you to get swindled out of your money by the government. There are booby traps within the system that are specifically targeting the new and naïve investor. For example, while the type of business that can be traded is fairly broad, the values of these two respective businesses need to be comparable to one another. If one business or property type is more successful than the one that it's being traded for, the government will tax you and you'll be left with a property that was less valuable than the one with which you started.

1031 Exchange Rule 3: Delaying Your Exchange is O.K.

Chances are, it's going to be pretty difficult to find someone who is going to want to buy the exact property that you own in exchange for the exact property that you desire. Due to this fact, it is possible to conduct three-party exchanges. This type of exchange is called a delayed exchange. You "sell" your property to someone who holds your money until he or she finds a replacement property for you to buy. The middleman in this scenario typically gets a cut from your exchange, so that may be one large deterrent from exchanging in this manner; however, it definitely does make it more likely that you will trade your property with the right investor and that you will find the best property to suit your needs.

Additionally, there are four catches associated with this type of exchange. The first one is that you only have forty-five days from the time you sell your property to the middleman or woman to signify in writing which replacement property you seek to obtain. The second is that you cannot receive the cash from your sale, as this will cause your exchange to be considered null in the eyes of the government at this point. Thirdly, in a delayed exchange, you are required to close your sale within six months. This parameter makes it seem as though there is a timeline on how "delayed" your delayed exchange can be. Lastly, let's say that you are trading a property, but the property that you're getting is less valuable than the property that you're giving away. To compensate for this, the other person within the trade has decided to give you cash so that you are receiving as much value as you are trading. The money that you receive from this sale must be taxed. Within the industry, this type of cash is commonly known as "boot".

These rules that have been outlined surrounding the 1031 Exchange only scratch the surface in terms of the nuances that lie within this tricky tax regulation. The best advice to give within the world of real estate trading is to study. There are definitely good beginner guidelines presented in this chapter, but if you walk away from this book knowing that real estate trading is the type of investing that you'd like to partake in, these facts are not enough. Many people who go the route of real estate trading hire professionals who know the ins and outs of the 1031 tax code. In addition to investing in property trading, investing in an expert who will keep you away from not only losing money but also potential jail time is more than a good idea. If you hire a professional, you will thank yourself later.

Chapter 7:
The Basics of Leveraging

If the wild world of real estate trading doesn't seem like it's for you, another type of investment strategy that might suit you better is the idea of leveraging. Leveraging is a technique where money is borrowed for an investment, with the hope that the returns on the investment will be greater than the interest that you're forced to pay on the borrowed money. It's helpful to look at a tangible example of this concept before delving deeper into how exactly real estate leveraging works. Let's say that you take a loan so that you can buy a new car. You take out a loan because you want to be flashy and decide to buy a new Mercedes. While the vehicle costs $100,000, you only give the salesman $20,000. This is only twenty percent of the total cost of the vehicle. Instead of driving around in a $20,000 car, you get to drive around in a $100,000 car for only $20,000 upfront. You look cooler and your wallet feels safe. Excluding the interest that's accruing on the other $80,000, this is a win-win for you.

If we take this example a step further, let's say that instead of driving around in your new $100,000 vehicle, you decide to immediately sell your Mercedes for $120,000. The economy is good at the time so your car sells for $120,000 in full. From a mathematical perspective, this means that you made back the entire $20,000 that you originally gave to the car dealership for the Mercedes in the first place. This $20,000 did not have interest attached to it. By using the concepts of leveraging you were able to get back one hundred percent of your investment on that car by selling it at a price of $120,000. If you look at this a different way, the concepts of leveraging become even clearer. Let's say that instead of taking out a loan and buying the car for $20,000, you decide to buy the car outright for $100,000. After you buy the car, you still decide to sell the car at the higher price of $120,000. In this scenario, because you did not take out a loan, your return on the car only ends up being ten percent of your original investment, rather than a full one hundred percent. By comparing these two scenarios, it's possible to see how leveraging can be beneficial to the investor.

If we expand this example even further to encompass real estate investing, the consequences of leveraging become even greater and distinct. Let's say that a real estate investor has $100,000 to spend on a property. If he or she were to buy property in full at a cost of $100,000, he or she would have to sell the property at a whopping price of $200,000, because only then would he or she see a one hundred percent return on the money that was originally invested. Contrastingly, an investor could instead make the choice to instead spend $20,000 as a down payment on five different properties. The rest of the money for each property would be bought with money that the investor borrowed from a bank. If the investor chose to do this instead of buy the property at $100,000 outright, each property would only have to be sold at $120,000 in order for the investor to break even. If the investor were lucky enough to sell all five properties at a price of $120,000, he or should would see one hundred percent of their original investment. As is seen in this example, by leveraging money against the multiple properties that the investor buys, it is not only easier to make a profit but also makes more sense from a mathematical perspective. What's more, if the investor were to hold onto these properties and rent them out to tenants instead of immediately sell them, the rent payments would most likely cover the monthly mortgage on each property. If the investor did the math correctly, he or she could make sure that the tenants on the property were covering the cost of not only the mortgage on the property, but also the interest that is being generated from the original loan that was taken out against the value of the home. In this way, the real estate investor is making even more money through the technique of leveraging.

In thinking about how to properly use leveraging to successfully maximize your profit margins within the real estate sector, it's important to check and double check how high your interest rates will be and whether or not the rates will be variable or fixed. With fixed variable interest rates, you have less to worry about because you know exactly how much the mortgage payment on the house will be each month. Take the time to figure out with your mortgage lender whether or not you have the appropriate funds to engage in leveraging activity. Additionally, it's important to note that the more properties you buy, the higher your interest rates will be. Often, a bank lender will stop giving a real estate investor money after he or she owns at least ten properties. Of course, it is possible to go to more than one bank in order to get the funds needed to invest in an additional property, but it's more important to make sure that you're able to keep your payments up-to-date, especially when deciding to go down the path of leveraging. Borrow too much money, and the result can be desolate bankruptcy.

Conclusion

Thank you again for reading this book!

I hope this book was able to help you to feel more knowledgeable about how real estate investing works and provided you with valuable strategies on how you can start to invest in real estate property. Through the discussion of various ways in which investing in real estate is possible, you should be able to choose which type of investment you are most interested in making. Even if you are interested in more than one approach, you should still consider prioritizing each type of investment. This way, you can start your investment portfolio in one category before moving into another. If you overwhelm yourself by moving into too many different areas at once, you are more likely to make mistakes from the start and end up losing money. As you become more versed in real estate investing, try to keep in mind the value of patience and that often, the longer you hold onto a property, the more value it accrues over time.

The next step is to plan your approach. If you already know which particular investment strategy you're going to use, begin gathering the information that you'll need to be successful in a given area. This includes verifying with your bank that the capital you need exists and acquiring documented proof of these funds. Additionally, if you have not already done so, it might be a good idea to see what local investment opportunities are available to you. If you can meet face-to-face with an investment group or interact with other people who are veterans in this field, you might be able to develop business relationships in real and significant ways.

Finally, if you enjoyed this book, please take the time to share your thoughts and post a review on Amazon. It'd be greatly appreciated!

Thank you and good luck!

Made in the USA
San Bernardino, CA
03 November 2016